31 Positive Communication Skills Devotional for Women

Published in the United States of America

Cover Design by Nick Tyra

Unless otherwise noted, Scripture quotations are taken from the Holy Bible, New International Version®, NIV®. Copyright © 1973, 1978, 1984, 2011 by Biblica, Inc.™ Used by permission of Zondervan. All rights reserved worldwide. www.zondervan.com

Scriptures marked ESV are from the ESV® Bible (The Holy Bible, English Standard Version®), copyright © 2001 by Crossway, a publishing ministry of Good News Publishers. Used by permission. All rights reserved.

Scriptures marked NLT are from Holy Bible, New Living Translation, copyright © 1996, 2004, 2007, 2013 by Tyndale House Foundation. Used by permission of Tyndale House Publishers, Inc., Carol Stream, Illinois 60188. All rights reserved.

Scriptures marked GW are from GOD'S WORD a copyrighted work of God's Word to the Nations. Quotations are used by permission. Copyright 1995 by God's Word to the Nations. All rights reserved.

Library of Congress Cataloging-in-Publication Data

Largent, Christy.

31 positive communication skills for women devotional: encouraging words to help you speak your truth with confidence / Christy Largent.

pages cm

Includes bible verse index

ISBN

1. Communication Skills - Religious aspects - Christianity. 2. Business Communication - Women. 3. Christian Devotionals.

31

Positive Communication Skills

Devotional for Women

*Encouraging Words to Help You
Speak your Truth with Confidence*

Christy Largent

Contents

Dedication

For Tom, Amelia and Graham. Thank you for helping me practice what I preach. You make my life complete. I love you.

Introduction

"Let the words of my mouth and the meditations of my heart be acceptable in your sight, oh Lord, my strength and my redeemer." – Psalms 19:14

When I went off to college I wanted to change the world. The way I was going to do this was by becoming the next Joan Lunden or Jane Pauley, (remember them!). I would be the one to shine the light of Christ in the darkness of 1980's culture, as a morning TV host.

Once I got to college I connected with a mentor, Cal Thomas, who suggested that the real change making in this world happened behind the scenes. He emphasized that writing the material that those personalities read was where I could really make an impact. So, being the typical pleaser that I was, I listened to Cal, changed my major from speech communications to political science and quickly lost focus on my dream.

Fast forward 30 years and in many ways it seems my life has come full circle. Although I'm not hosting a show on national TV, I am a host of a local public TV talk show. I'm writing through the vehicle of my blog, but most important of all, I found my change-making vehicle by becoming a humorist and professional speaker helping people realize their potential to live purposeful, positive lives.

I help people create a life of positive connection and help them cultivate purposeful living. And that's what life is all about anyway, isn't it? When you learn how to create positive connections, you are building healthy, happy relationships. You are learning how to love people in the way they need to be loved.

You are encouraging others to create healthy, vibrant relationships of their own. When you begin cultivating a life of meaning and purpose, your life changes. And slowly, one skill, one idea, one tool at a time, the world changes for the better.

When I thought of putting together a resource on communication skills, I immediately wanted to tie it into a devotional format. Because the truth is, real change only happens when it happens from your heart. And that takes more than just desire and effort. That actually takes the supernatural work of the Holy Spirit.

So, I give you 31 days' worth of suggestions, skills and ideas you can immediately implement so that you will be able to overcome the obstacles of difficult communication and build deep, meaningful relationships. Or at least get on the journey. The verses I've included will help you hear what God says on the subject, so that you can take it to a deeper level. Ponder these verses. Think about them in context of the skill they are connected with. Ask the Lord to show you how you can implement these ideas into your life.

If you would like to share your thoughts with more than just me, please leave a review on Amazon. I'd appreciate it more than you know.

My prayer for you is all the success you desire as you learn to communicate more clearly, confidently and with the power of the Holy Spirit, even more courageously. Let's go change the world together!

I'd love to hear how these concepts are working for you. Please leave me feedback at my website: **www.christylargent.com** or email me directly at **christylargentspeaker@gmail.com.**

First Impressions

"So whether you eat or drink or whatever you do, do it all
for the glory of God. Do not cause anyone to stumble,
whether Jews, Greeks or the church of God — even as I try
to please everybody in every way. For I am not seeking my
own good but the good of many, so that they may be
saved." – 1 Corinthians 10:31-33

The first thing I noticed were the shoes. Camouflage, with a six-inch heel, they were showstoppers. Darling. Definite. Daring! It was the first day of kindergarten roundup and I knew nobody. But right after I noticed the shoes, I noticed the lady wearing them. She had a big smile on her face and she was laughing with her son. When she saw me watching them, she directed her smile my way and stretched out her hand. "Hi, I'm Maureen," she said. "Hi, I'm Christy, I like your shoes." And a friendship was born.

Not only were we two of the most "seasoned" mothers at that roundup, ahem, but despite the height of that shoe heel, we were also kindred spirits. Over the intervening six years, I'm happy to say my first impression of Maureen was spot on. She is darling. She is definite. She is daring!

The statistics say we have about seven seconds to make a first impression. Maureen did a lot of things right to create a positive first impression with me. She's a business owner and she knows the power of impact. Here are a few things you can do to get off on the right foot. Ahem.

1) Stand up straight and smile. There's something about a smile that invites a positive response. You immediately signal you are friendly and open and ready to start something good.

2) Stick out your right hand, say your name and give a nice handshake. You can almost never go wrong by initiating the handshake. In American culture, a handshake is a universal clue that you want to get the conversation started.

3) Lean towards the person you are meeting. Sheryl Sandberg had it right when she said "Lean In." Your body will send your message of interest loud and clear before you even say a word.

4) Look them in the eye. As I'm training my kids how to meet new people, the hardest thing for them to understand is the power of looking the other person in the eye. They want to hang their head and mumble. Each time, I gently encourage them to lift their head and look the other person in the eye as they are introducing themselves.

5) Speak up. When you say your name, say it clearly. Nothing is worse than having to ask, "What was your name again?" Make sure, that as you introduce

yourself, you are projecting your voice towards the listener.

The bottom line is that creating an awesome first impression is a lot easier than you might think. It's really all about the other person. When you ask yourself, "How can I give them what they need so they feel comfortable entering into a conversation with me?" you're on the right track.

Interesting, isn't it. When we take our eyes off ourselves and put them on the other person, we're bound to win. Oh, and awesome shoes will always help too.

Taking it Deeper:

What can you do intentionally to create a positive first impression? What is your experience with this? Have you ever been wrong with a first impression? How did it affect your relationship with the person? Do you think you create a positive impression? If not, what's holding you back?

Day 2

Charisma 101

> *"Nothing should be done because of pride or thinking about yourself. Think of other people as more important than yourself."* – Philippians 2:3 (NLT)

Who do you think of as the most charismatic person you know? My guess is that it's someone who is confident, positive, widely read, engaging and encouraging. They are someone who seems to light up a room when they enter, and when they leave, everything is just a little bit dimmer.

People sometimes say charisma is something you're either born with or you're not. I think it's even simpler than that. Although it may be easier for some people than others, the reality is that most people who are perceived as having charisma actually do certain things that create that perception. Curious?

Here are my Top 5 hallmarks of a charismatic person:

1) **Confidence.** They don't apologize for being them-selves. They embrace it. They don't think they're too

short, too tall, too fat, too thin, too bald, too much hair, too old, too young. They've stopped all that nonsense cold. Charismatic people know that the best version of me, is me! So they embrace it. And then they own it. Confidence is contagious. That's charismatic.

2) **Ask questions.** One of the most noticeable attributes of a charismatic person is that they make *you* feel like you are special. They are really INTO you. They don't just rattle on about how awesome they are, they focus on you and ask you questions about yourself. They ask open ended questions (more on that in a later reading) and wait eagerly for your answer. Get really good as asking questions. That's charismatic.

3) **Listen well.** Another striking quality of charismatic people is how well they listen. When you are talking, they are not busy formulating answers or thinking of the next question (remember, they are confident). Instead, they are 100% focused on you as you answer their questions. They listen for ways to connect and relate. Become a good listener. That's charismatic.

4) **Have something interesting to say.** A key element of a charismatic person is how they seem to always have an engaging tidbit to share. They pay attention to the world, and others are interested in their observations. They read books, blogs, and newspapers. They listen to podcasts and radio and even occasionally go to movies or watch TV. So when it's time to talk, they're interesting. That's charismatic.

5) **Laugh at yourself.** Don't take yourself so serious-ly! Charismatic people understand the power of laughter and the first joke is always on them. So learn how to be funny and start with yourself. Look for the humor in

daily life and share. Everyone loves to laugh, and charismatic people live and lead with laughter. That's charismatic.

Can you tell that the magic secret to charisma is this secret idea..."Seek to be interested more than interesting." That's it. That's the secret. All these things I've listed are really ways to show you are interested in others. Simple. Easy to practice. You can do it. That's charismatic.

> ### *Taking it Deeper:*
> What do you think makes someone charismatic? How do you tap into your own charisma to build relationships? What can you work on to strengthen this skill?

Day 3

Your Communication Image

"In the same way, if you don't speak in a way that can be understood, how will anyone know what you are saying? You will be talking into thin air."

– 1 Corinthians 4:19 (GW)

I have a friend who routinely rambles when she has a story to share. When she needs help with a project, she always gives a five-minute explanation for why she is asking. She is rarely clear on what she wants, and drops hints, hoping I will pick up her true meaning. It's exhausting! And I can't help but think she carries this propensity to her work as well. In fact, she is frequently frustrated because she is passed up for promotions and overlooked when exciting new projects become available. Could it be her vague, apologetic communication style is being projected onto her abilities?

19

My guess is that you would really like to create a positive and professional image with your words whether you are CEO of a large corporation or CEO of your home. With that in mind, if you want to be perceived as a positive communicator, here are 3 key suggestions:

1. Be clear. Ambiguity may have its place in poetry or novels, but for interpersonal communication ambiguity leads to misunderstandings. If you want something accomplished, say it in terms that are clear and definite. Don't beat around the bush.

For Example:
Unclear: "I could sure use some help around here."
Clear: "Please clear the table, put the dishes in the dishwasher and take out the trash."
Ask: How can I make my conversation clearer?

2. Be concise. There's nothing worse than someone who rambles on and on and on and on and... well, you get the picture. Sometimes we ramble because we don't know what to say or are nervous about giving an answer we don't want to give. Just spit it out.

For Example:
Rambling: "If it's possible, and you're not too busy, and I know you really have a lot to do, but I could really use your help, if you could just take a sec and look at this project and see if I'm on the right track, because it's the first time I've done anything like this, if it's not too much trouble."
Concise: "Do you have five minutes? There's a project I'd like to get your input on."
Ask: How can I be more concise?

3. Be committed. Don't hedge. A hedge, according to Phyllis Mindell, a recognized expert on women and language, is when you "hide behind words, refuse to commit oneself." Women tend to do this more than men. These words don't add meaning, they just add to the sentence - in an effort to soften the sentence. When you commit to clear, concise communication, you will be able to omit these.

For Example:
Hedging: "Well, I would really like us to start the meeting at 8:00 am, if it's not too inconvenient for everyone."
Committed: "The meeting starts at 8:00 am, and I expect everyone to attend.
Ask: What words can I omit and still retain the meaning?

It's not easy to speak with clarity and intention. I want to encourage you to put these three ideas into practice and see if you get better results. I know you will enjoy creating a positive, professional communication image.

Taking it Deeper:
Are you doing your best to create communication that is clear, concise and committed? Do you have a bad habit of muddling up conversations? How can you start implementing these ideas today?

Day 4

Create Your Best Voice

"She speaks with wisdom and faithful instruction is on her tongue." – Proverbs 31:26

She came up to me after class and waited in line to visit. My first impression of her was really good. She was dressed professionally and had a nice smile and really cute hair. She had a charming smile. And then she opened her mouth and began to speak. Oh. My... Disaster! It was as if I were speaking with a 10-year-old excited about her first trip to Disneyland. Breathy. Fast. High pitched. Run-on sentences. Yikes!

The way you say something has even more impact than the words you speak. Your delivery will either make or break your communication. God gave you the vocal chords and physical realities you are working with—it's up to you to work with these and hone your voice into a melodious instrument.

Here are three main areas to develop in order to be a powerful communicator:

1. Volume - The amount of sound that is produced

Too loud: You hear Loud Lucinda from clear across the room. Oblivious to being obnoxious, she thinks louder is better. Maybe she has a hearing problem. Or maybe she's just excited. Or maybe she just wants everyone to notice her. Regardless, too loud is just plain wrong.

Too soft: Sally Softie looks and sounds like she is wrapped in pink cotton. She whispers her thoughts as if she's afraid of your response. She never notices how hard you are straining to hear her words, or that you eventually just give up in frustration and start nodding your head looking in vain for a way to escape the conversation. Too soft hurts too.

Just right: Just right Janie is very aware that different situations require different volumes. She will raise her voice for impact or lower to attract interest. She knows that volume is a tool that works best when it is varied. She makes sure to have a nice mixture of both loud and soft and that each is used both skillfully and appropriately.

2. Pitch - Pitch is technically defined as the "rate of vibration of the vocal folds"

Too high: The more vibrations the higher the tone. A higher voice is frequently discounted or minimized as being too "childlike" to be of value. (I have to work on not being too high pitched—especially when I'm excited!)

Too low: A lower tone is commonly recognized as more competent and knowledgeable. Although we women may want to sound like Lauren Bacall, for most of us, that won't be an option. People who have super low voices can be perceived as being too sexual and not serious.

Just right: Find your natural spot. If it's in the upper middle range, go lower. Lower voices are perceived as voices of authority, so it's in our best interest to make an effort to modulate our pitches so that they are still natural, but as low as feels comfortable. Aim for the lower middle range.

3. Rate - How fast or slowly we speak

Too fast: Super excited and young and happy. Think of your kindergartener spilling the beans about an upcoming birthday party the minute he gets in the car after school. Too fast minimizes the value of your information.

Too slow: One word. Boring. Slow and steady is a good formula for saving money, it's the kiss of death when speaking. Even though slow speech can indicate thoughtfulness, be careful about going too slowly.

Just right: We normally speak at about 125 words per minute. Audio books are about 150-160 words per minute (they have to keep your attention) and auctioneers are off the charts at double that. Just right is somewhere between 110 and 150 depending on the situation. As with the other elements, keep it appropriate and you'll be in a good spot.

The best way to find out how you are doing in these areas is to record yourself and listen back. Once you get over the staggering "yuck" of listening to yourself, you'll get some helpful insights into where you can tweak things to create your perfect voice.

Taking it Deeper:
Is your voice helping or hurting your message? Can you think of a time when someone dismissed what you said because of how you said it? Which of these areas do you need to work on to become a more effective communicator?

It's How You Say It

> *"A gentle answer turns away wrath, but a harsh word stirs up anger."* – Proverbs 15:1

When I asked the children for an example of how a "Type A - Driver - Red Choleric" might say something, a little 8-year-old girl excitedly raised her hand. "I know, I know," she exclaimed. "OK," I laughed, "come on up here and show us how it would look and sound." So she jumped out of her chair and raced to the front of the room. She planted her feet and put one hand on her hip. Cocking her head and leaning forward she shook the finger of the other hand with each word she spoke. "I TOLD you to CLEAN YOUR ROOM!" We all laughed as her mother flushed dark red and slowly sunk deeper into her chair.

How many times have you heard the phrase, "It's not what you say, it's how you say it"? It seems like a million times. But guess what, it's true! Today I want to help you fine tune your pitch and tone. It's so important because most of the time, as evidenced by the story above, tone dictates meaning. Let's look at some examples of tone in action...

Monotone Mary: Mary never gets very excited about anything. Her pitch rarely varies more than a few levels in either direction and her volume stays specifically just below the medium level. When she talks, it's easy to forget what she said immediately after she says it because everything sounds the same. You have to guess what's most important to her because there's no emphasis in her speech. She's kind of like that recorded message at the airport that warns you not to leave your baggage unattended. Easy to ignore and relegate into background noise.

Sarcastic Susan: Susan's the master of double meanings. When she asks a question or gives a comment, the thick sarcastic tone usually causes you to doubt how she wants you to answer. Susan thinks she's funny because of her sarcastic "wit" but her negative commentary is very wearing. In meetings, she's free with inflection-laden suggestions, usually at the expense of another. When she's confronted about her comments, she always denies she said anything wrong. And let's face it, technically, the words were fine; it was the sarcasm suffocating them that stopped productive communication.

Excitable Emily: Emily is always excited about everything! You hear her before you see her! There are lots of exclamation points in her delivery! Her volume is as high as her energy! She emphasizes various words to make her points, and there are a lot of points to make! She tends to be positive, but hasn't come to understand that too much of a good thing is too much! She makes you tired. You tune her out because it's ALL! TOO! MUCH!!

Conversational Callie: Callie is a master communicator. She uses a variety of pitches and volumes when she speaks. She draws you in. Her lower and slower tone of voice attracts your attention…and then she delivers her message with power and humor. She knows that variety is truly the spice of life, and when she speaks she harnesses that variety so you stay engaged. Rarely does she speak with sarcasm, so if the joke is on someone, it's on herself. You like being around Callie because she uses her tone to build up others and strengthen her message.

I hope these examples have reminded you of what kind of tone can be most effective. Notice your own tone, and ask yourself if you are communicating the way you really want to, or if you've fallen into some bad habits.

> **Taking it Deeper:**
> Which of these do you think you most closely resemble? What are some ways you can become more like Callie? Do you think your style helps or hinders your communication?

Flourish

"Let your speech always be gracious, seasoned with salt, so that you may know how you ought to answer each person." – Colossians 4:6 ESV

Do you know you are a gardener? Every day you have the opportunity to cultivate a relational garden that will flourish. A flourishing garden is a safe environment and it promotes clear, honest and productive communication. Take the mini-quiz and see how your garden is flourishing.

Quiz

1) Has anyone ever told you they "didn't know how you would take it," so they avoided telling you important information until after the fact?

2) Do you have difficulty giving people a second chance, because you expect perfection the first time?

3) Have you ever brought up something someone said a long time ago and used it in a current conversation to make your point?

If you answered yes to any of these questions, following are a few reminders of the elements required for a safe and healthy garden that fosters positive communication.

Soil - Authenticity. How authentic are you? Are you the same person regardless of the situation? As a leader, do you operate the same way with your staff as you do with your peers? Do you share your own struggles and challenges with your team, or do you create a façade of perfection? If you struggle with showing your true self, then you need to focus on being Authentic. It's the foundation.

Water - Give Grace. Grace means "Undeserved favor performed out of your good will." Do you give others the benefit of the doubt or do you wait for them to flub up so you can point out their error? Do you choose to give people second chances? This doesn't mean you have unhealthy boundaries. It's just you accept that people are flawed, and you're willing to allow them to be less than perfect, and maybe even help them recover when they have failed. Healthy environments require finding ways to give grace, just like water, daily.

Fertilize - Encourage Communication. When you encourage communication, people feel safe talking with you. They know conversations are confidential. They know you listen for meaning, not just to gain information to use later. You also recognize that sometimes people just have to verbally process in order for them to synthesize the information they have received. You are also willing to share of yourself. You're not closed and unwilling to reveal yourself to them. Communication flows both ways.

Making sure to include these elements into your everyday environment is hard work. But it's worth it when you begin to see your relationships blossom and grow strong so that that not only will they withstand life's stresses, but will flourish in the midst of them.

> ### *Taking it Deeper:*
> What kind of communication environment are you cultivating? Are you intentional with any of these 3 key elements? What are some practical behaviors you can do right now to improve your relationships?

Day 7

The Power of Positive

"Finally, brothers, whatever is true, whatever is honorable, whatever is just, whatever is pure, whatever is lovely, whatever is commendable, if there is any excellent, if there is anything worthy of praise, think about these things."
Philippians 4:8 ESV

My girlfriend is a kindergarten teacher in a charter school. Several years ago she was really having trouble with one little guy. So early in October she pulled him aside and said, "Buddy, I need your help. You are the smartest kid in this class, and I need you to help me show the other kids how to behave. I need you to be my biggest helper because you can be!"

And do you know, his behavior problems "magically" disappeared, and she ended up having a great year...with the whole class. You see, she had the same conversation with each student, and they all rose to her vision and expectations for them. In the business world, we call this using Praise, Rewards and

Recognition to develop your people. At home, I call it helping myself stay sane.

Do you realize people respond to your expectations? In study after study, scientists have observed the power of positive expectations. So whether you need this technique at home or work or both, let's take a look at how you can bring out the best with positive expectations.

Praise: Look for positives and respond. Once, while I was doing a training in Arkansas, a supervisor from the Little Debbie factory raised her hand and said, "My workers are working hard at a difficult and repetitive job on an assembly line. I always like to catch 'em doing something right!" You can bet she had motivated and empowered workers.

In order to come across as authentic with your praise, make sure it is both sincere and specific. People believe you are sincere with your praise when you are specific. For example, if you tell your employee, "I really appreciate you. I know you've put in a lot of extra time on this project and I appreciate it. Thank you for your hard work and your attention to detail." Your employee will be energized and motivated to do even more. And I must add, with certain employees, a letter spelling out this praise will be most highly valued of all.

We know people work harder for praises than raises. Most importantly though, they will know you sincerely appreciate them...you told them so with Praise.

Recognition and Rewards: Create an environment for people to look good! When you walk in the door of the Arbonne International headquarters, almost the first thing you see is a huge wall filled with pictures of top achievers in the company. These achievers are recognized for their accomplishments.

Focus positive attention on the quality of work and keep it there. My 5th grade daughter is intensely focused on getting all her homework finished on time, and finished perfectly so she can participate in her teacher's "Friday Rewards." And the even bigger goal is the "Perfect week, Perfect month" reward. And on top of that, each test holds the potential of receiving a "Big Cookie" for a 98% or higher on the test. Her teacher has tapped into the power of recognition and rewards for her 4th and 5th graders.

There are all kinds of ways you can incorporate Praise, Recognition and Rewards into your communication life. If you're short on ideas, I recommend a book called *The Carrot Principle: How the Best Managers Use Recognition to Engage Their People, Retain Talent, and Accelerate Performance* by Adrian Gostick and Chester Elton. It's loaded with great ideas you can implement immediately both at work and home.

This is a perfect time to re-commit to the power of positive. Love the people in your life this way. They will thank you and both of you will be better for it.

Taking it Deeper:

Do you find it easy to focus on the positive this way? What are some good ways you have given praise, recognition and rewards? How can you focus on all the good things God gives us? Check out Crystal Paine's (Money Saving Mom) *Choose Gratitude: Blessings Journal.* There's nothing like focusing on the good to help you stay positive and this journal will keep you on the right track.

Day 8

Listen With Your Heart

"Know this, my beloved brothers (and sisters): let every person be quick to hear, slow to speak, slow to anger."
James 1:19 ESV

It was the summer of 1984 and I was an intern in Washington D.C. My job included weekly briefings at the White House, research that would be presented to the Supreme Court and now this! I, along with three others, was waiting to be ushered in to take a private meeting with Congressman Jack Kemp. Former professional football player, friend and advisor of presidents, and now, meet-er of interns! I had to pinch myself.

Our conversation got off to a good start with a discussion of current events. The talk moved to the problem of the Sandinistas in Nicaragua and in those days before the Iran Contra affair became known to all, it was natural to ask the Congressman what ideas he had for dealing with them. When he gave his answer, I immediately piped up with, "But why do you think that would work when we've tried it before and it failed?" He immediately leaned way back in his chair, crossed his arms behind his reclining head, swung his crossed legs up onto the top of his desk and fired back, "What do you think we should do?" Clearly, he was not interested in my answer, nor was he receptive to anything I might have to say. Considering I was just 20 and more than a little intimidated by this show of "manliness" I quickly responded, "I don't know, you're the Congressman."

Needless to say, that was the end of that discussion and we moved on to other topics and the meeting was over not long after. What happened there was a beautiful display of how NOT to listen. Congressman Kemp's dramatic body language put form to his feelings. He had no interest in meeting with us or hearing what we had to say. So since he couldn't say that to his scheduler, he dramatically let us know we needed to get moving along.

So, how do you avoid the same mistake in Listening? I believe there are 3 key things you can do to be an active listener.

The first and most important is to Focus. The second and third (follow and feedback) we will look at tomorrow.

Key #1 ~ Focus: Focus with your body first and then your mind. This is how you do it: Uncross your arms and legs. If you are sitting, lean slightly forward, about seven degrees. When your body is open and you're tilted slightly forward towards the speaker, it conveys you are interested in what the other person has to say. This posture also helps you focus your mind on the immediate conversation. Your mind will be less likely to wander to your grocery list, or who is picking up the kids from school, or what you are going to do with that problem employee. Instead, you'll be laser focused on the conversation. Note: do not do this forward lean if you are standing—people will move away from you because you'll be invading their space.

Oftentimes people are resistant to truly focusing during a conversation. I think that's because it's much easier to stay distant when you're only half-way invested in the conversation. When you fully focus, you run the risk of becoming vulnerable as they share their vulnerability with you. Think about it. That's a scary place to be. But oh, so worth it! Let's use focus to really listen with our hearts.

> ### *Taking it Deeper:*
> Do you focus when you are listening or are you easily distracted? When you do focus, do you give yourself permission to respond authentically and with vulnerability? What are the things that distract you? How can you eliminate them and get focused?

Day 9

Listening in Action

"Let the wise listen and add to their learning, and let the discerning get guidance." – Proverbs 1:5

I want you to stop right now, close your eyes and picture the person you would consider to be the best listener you know. What are the characteristics that come to mind? My guess is that not only do they give you their intent focus, as we talked about yesterday, but they also do the two things I'm going to discuss today. They follow and they give you appropriate feedback. Let's look a little deeper.

Key #2 ~ Follow: Follow first with silence and then with open-ended questions. Think back to your favorite listener. Let me ask you, does the person who came to mind give you lots and lots of space around your sentences? Do they let you have a pause at the end of your thoughts? I'll bet they do. That's called following with silence. That's probably the main reason you think of them as a great listener too.

You can do this too. During a conversation, consciously be quiet and allow a small space to follow after the person you listening to says something. (I try for three seconds.) A funny thing will happen when you do this. Either they realize they have more to say—and say it, or they're finished with their thought and they're waiting for your follow-up. As you are actively listening, if they don't speak after 3 seconds, you can then follow up with an open-ended question. That is, a question that cannot be answered with a yes or no answer. This will keep the conversation moving forward and they will feel heard.

Key #3 ~ Feedback: This is the final step you can do when you are an active listener. You can give feedback by reflecting with your body and reflecting with your words. Think of the concept of mirroring the person speaking. They tilt their head, you tilt your head. They lean right, you lean left. Basically, you're matching their movements.

Did you know that people like people who are "like themselves?" Think of your best friends. Aren't they similar to you in many ways? The same thing holds true with listening. People like to engage in conversation with people who are "like them." Now, don't be a dork! This isn't the game my 2nd grader played tonight at the dinner table where he mimicked my every word and behavior! Just do it gently with your body and then with your words. When they comment, "We're going to Hawaii for our vacation." You can reply, "Oh, so you're going to Hawaii, how exciting!" This confirms for them that you are listening and interested. You show that you are interested by giving them this verbal reflection.

3 Keys ~ Focus, Follow and Feedback. Three simple steps to energize yourself towards Active Listening. Try it and see what happens. I guarantee, when you commit to this behavior, you'll see deepened relationships and more productive communication.

> ### *Taking it Deeper:*
> Which of these three types of active listening behaviors are your favorite to use? To be the recipient of? What do you think really keeps you from doing your best listening?

A Widespread Plague

"Do not speak to a fool, for he will scorn the wisdom of your words." – Proverbs 23:9

I only have to say one word and you know exactly what I'm talking about. Immediately, you picture all the pain, sorrow and fear this word evokes. I really don't even need to say "Ebola" because you already know what I'm talking about. It's bad news in its every crevice.

Did you know that in the world of communication and relationships there is also a plague? It is a plague that goes largely unnamed and unchecked - a plague that affects virtually every one of us. Despite its alarming range, there are not many of us who are immune to it and its devastating effects. Most of us have even been guilty, at some point, of not only being a carrier of this disease - but of actively passing it on to someone else! What is it you ask?

The problem is the plague of giving unsolicited advice.

Are you a carrier? Have you been infected? Or have you been inoculated just enough to make you immune to it from others, but still wickedly powerful in your ability to spread its devastation? Not sure? Then read on...

Definition: Unsolicited Advice is when you offer your opinions, suggestions or ideas to someone about something they are doing or planning, before they ask for your input. I know most of us have excellent motives when we offer up these little truffles and tidbits of testimony. But if you are brutally honest with yourself, you'll recognize how frequently your unrequested suggestions are rebuffed or brushed away, not to mention met with defensiveness and ultimately rejection. So, what's the cure?

Ask Yourself: What gives me the right? This cure was found in the extremely helpful book by Doris Wild Helmering, *Being Ok Just Isn't Enough: The Power of Self-Discovery*. Ms. Helmering suggests that this is the first question you should ask before you open your mouth.

Again, ask yourself...What gives me the right to tell my friend where to park as we're circling the mall looking for a parking spot? What gives me the right to tell my co-worker how to "more effectively" do the project he's working on? Or how about this...What gives me the right to tell my husband how to trim the bushes?

Ooooh! Got your attention on that last one didn't I? You probably responded, "But I have the right because it's my yard too!" And you would be correct. You do have the right. In tomorrow's reading, I'll elaborate on how to process this—when you do have the right to give unsolicited advice. The question becomes...should you? I propose that when you don't have the right, that is, it's none of your business, you keep your mouth shut and your opinions to yourself. But when you do have the right. I also propose you ask yourself a few questions before you open your mouth and spout your opinion or suggestion. Check out tomorrow for what those questions are...

> ### *Taking it Deeper:*
> Do you give unsolicited advice? What tempts you to do it? How can you keep yourself from doling out advice like candy? What has been the reaction of others when you have done this in the past? Is that the reaction you had hoped for?

Day 11

Stopping the Plague

"A fool finds no pleasure in understanding but delights in airing his own opinions." – Proverbs 18:2

What gives you the right? That's the question I challenged you with previously as we talked about giving Unsolicited Advice. Do you have the right to comment? If not, then don't. If you do, however, as when I asked "what gives you the right to tell your husband how to trim the bushes?" then it's a different story.

Here's where it gets a bit tricky. Ask yourself this. What if trimming the bushes was one of the biggest thrills in your husband's life? Do you still have the right? And, what if each time he trimmed the bushes, they died. Yes, that's right. Dead. Brown. Kaput. As in, you have to pull them out and start over. Do you still have the right? Yes! (By the way, if it gets this bad, you must transition from mere unsolicited advice to a full-blown strategy of assertive dialogue—but that's another day's discussion.)

Even so, and especially when you have the right, before you open your mouth, ask yourself, "Is it in the best interest of the relationship for me to give this unsolicited advice?" If not, then keep quiet.

I can't emphasize this technique enough. If they don't ask, don't tell. Shhhh. Bite your tongue. Hum a tune. Try anything you can to stay silent and keep from transmitting the disease!

I admit this is a "hot button" topic for me. In fact, let me be authentic with you and make a confession...I'm in recovery. That's right; I am a recovering unsolicited advice giver. I grew up in a family where we felt *compelled* with a moral obligation to pass on our wisdom to anyone we saw doing something differently (i.e., not our way) than we thought it should be done. This propensity to participate in the plague has caused me untold misery and compounded problems - all because I never realized the destruction I was sowing. You'll be relieved to know I am in recovery, the cure is working, and I'm well on my way to a total healing.

But back to you. What stage are you in? Denial? Are you carrying the plague with you, bringing irritation and alienation to everyone you come in contact with? Or are you willing to start and work the steps of recovery by resolving to practice the cure?

Remember, before you speak up, ask yourself these two questions:
1) What gives me the right?
   and then,
2) Even if I have the right, is it in the best interest of the relationship?

There's no easy answer here, and if you struggle with this I suggest you give these steps a try. I know from experience, it's so much more rewarding and positive for a relationship when you can stay quiet, build relationship and interestingly enough, often the person you most want to help will end up coming to you and asking for advice. And then you can give it to your heart's content. Voila!

Taking it Deeper:

Do you give unsolicited advice? Have you tried these solutions? How do you think your relationships would benefit if you stayed quiet and waited to be asked before you gave your opinion?

Day 12

Squash That Negativity Bug

"Be joyful always; pray continually; give thanks in all circumstances, for this is God's will for you in Christ Jesus." – 1 Thessalonians 5:16-18

"Oh no, that project will never work." "Why do they always expect us to do the impossible?" "You know the clients will hate it." "He's so sick, he'll probably die soon."

Have you heard any of these phrases lately? Negative, energy sucking, relationship tearing, and motivation zapping phrases seem to be all the vogue. And it's kind of hard not to be negative when you read the paper, listen to the radio, and watch the news. Holy cow! Have things in this world ever been worse?

I'm going to suggest three simple ideas to keep you from letting that negativity bug get you down. They're simple. But they work. Let's take a closer look.

1) Commit to yourself not to be one of the negative ones in your environment. This is easier said than done, but "NO

NEGATIVE" should be your internal command. When you're tempted to chime in to a negative discussion or make a negative comment, remind yourself of your commitment. You can either say nothing, or better yet, reframe it so you have something positive to say.

2) Determine you will look for the good in every situation. It's amazing how this small choice can change your outcomes. I think my Dad is a great example of someone who finds the good in every situation. In 2003 he was diagnosed with stage two colon cancer. Surgery removed all the cancer, but his physicians recommended chemotherapy. As he was sitting in his home office on the morning of his first treatment, my Mother asked if she could do anything to help him get ready. With a bright voice and shiny eyes, my Dad replied, "I don't think so. I've got the new Clive Cussler book I've been wanting to read and the brand new Straight Ahead Big Band CD I've been wanting to listen to. You know, I've never done anything like this before. I think this could be kind of fun!"

Yes, that's right, FUN. Wow! What an attitude.

Before you say, how ridiculous to be so positive and light hearted about something so serious, stop a minute and think. No matter the outcome, wouldn't it make your time pass more enjoyably if you had a positive outlook rather than a negative one? Study after study shows the importance of a positive outlook on outcomes. Interestingly enough, today my Dad is a fit, healthy 75. Better than before and cancer free. I'm thankful.

I know many people do have negative outcomes even with a positive outlook. I have a friend who just lost her father to cancer, and I don't know of anyone who had a more positive spirit and deeply felt faith. Bad things happen. But the idea here is to look for the good no matter how bad the situation. It will benefit you and others. And who knows, it might even positively affect your outcome.

3) Get back on the positive wagon. We all succumb to negativity at one time or another. So the real success comes in recommitting yourself to a positive outlook so you can have a life of joy. If there's a deeper problem, and you find yourself living in negativity, I'd encourage you to get to a health care provider ASAP so you can get some help climbing out of the pit. Go for a walk, listen to some favorite music, jump on the trampoline with your kids. Do what you can to climb back on that wagon. Life is too short to spend it bound up in negativity.

I hope these reminders will help you when you find yourself tempted to get negative.

Taking it Deeper:
How do you overcome negativity? Do you find it difficult to see the positive side? How can you turn yourself around from negative to positive? What are your secret weapons in this battle?

How To Say No (Nicely)

"If any of you lacks wisdom, let him ask God, who gives generously to all without reproach, and it will be given him." – James 1:5 ESV

I got the call right when I was packing for a trip. I was familiar with the question even though I barely knew the speaker. "Can you join our committee?" she asked. And silly me. I fell into it for a whole bunch of reasons I'll save for later discussion. I heard myself saying "yes" when both my head and heart were screaming "NO!"

Do you have trouble saying the 'N' word? Do you find that because you can't say NO, you end up involved in all sorts of things you don't really want to do? Or are you one of those people who has no difficulty saying No. So much so, that people perceive you as self-centered and not a team player? If you can relate to either of these, read on.

Following is the first of three ways to say *No*. Using these ideas will help you build relationships rather than put a strain on them, while still making sure you end up doing only, and exactly, what you want to do.

The 3x5 No. Use this with someone you supervise, including your teenager! Here's an example. Your daughter comes to you and says, "Mother, I have to get this $300.00 purse, and I have to get it now!" Now you know that a $300 purse is not in the budget no way, no how, but you don't want to say "NO!" once again. (Or if you are like I am, say "Are you out of your cotton-pickin' mind?") Ahem...

Instead, here's how you handle it. "Sweetheart," you reply, "I want you to have this beautiful purse. It's gorgeous and stylish and I can see exactly why you want it. My problem is that a $300 purse for you is not in our family budget. Here's what I would like you to do. Take this 3x5 card." (Hand it to her.) "On one side you can write $300.00 purse and on the other side, I want you to list all the ways you can think of to pay for this $300.00 purse. When the card is full of ideas, I want you to bring it back to me and we can discuss the options."

The amazing thing about this method is how creative people can be when they really want something. Your daughter will come up with all sorts of terrific ideas you would have never thought of ~ and because it's her idea, she can't complain about it later. You will want to try this with your employee the next time they get negative about your solution to a problem. Ask them to come up with alternatives and watch the positive energy rise. Reminder—don't use this one with your boss!)

This 3x5 No is a very empowering way to teach problem solving skills. It's also a great way to keep the environment positive and pro-active. Tomorrow we will look at two more powerful suggestions. Now, excuse me please, I have a call to make. There's a committee I've got to go extricate myself from...

Taking it Deeper:

Do you have difficulty saying No? How clearly do you define your own boundaries? How much of your inability to say no comes from not having a clear picture of what you should be doing?

Day 14

More Skills For Saying No Nicely

"Do not be anxious about anything, but in everything, by prayer and petition, with thanksgiving, present yur requests to God. And the peace of God, which transcends all understanding, will guard your hearts and your minds in Christ Jesus." – Philippians 4:6-7

Did you try the 3x5 No? If so, good for you! If not...well, here are two more ways to say No, nicely. Maybe one of these will work for you.

The Priority No. This is the one you use with your boss. When she comes running to you and asks you to drop what you're doing and get to work immediately on this newer, higher priority project, here's what you do. Calmly pull out your list of priorities (discussed with and approved by your boss at the beginning of the current week), and ask her which of these other, prioritized items, she would like you to take off the list so that you can add her new priority project.

This little ploy will remind your boss that you are working off a priority list, and will either cause her to a) go find someone else to do the job, someone who is not working off a priority list, or b) re-think and re-assign the planned-on projects. Either way, you are in a good spot because you're sticking to the projects as planned, and you won't get penalized later for not finishing your priority list.

The one thing the Priority No requires is...yes, you guessed it...Priorities! Even if you work in an environment where priorities are not discussed—or things are unorganized and randomly worked on, you personally, need priorities. Take this opportunity to review what you are doing and make sure you are on track to reach your goals. In order to reach your goals, my guess is that you'll need to set priorities. I love this method of saying no because it always pulls me back to what's really important. Now, I just have to remember to use it! :)

The Full Plate No. This is the one you use with your friends and co-workers when they want to rope you into another "good cause" for which you really don't have time. For example, for the past 5 years you have enjoyed organizing the office holiday party. This year, however, you have begun taking night classes and you are too overloaded to organize the party. So, when they ask you about organizing the party again this year, you simply say, "Thank you for asking, however, my plate is really full right now, I'm going to have to pass on organizing the party this year."

Notice how simple this is! No long list of reasons or excuses, just a simple "no thank you." It's a clean and easy get-away, and leaves everyone feeling positive. This Full Plate No leaves you feeling empowered as you draw clear boundaries, and leaves the other person impressed you were able to clearly express your desires.

If saying No is a difficult area for you, the first thing I want to suggest is you really pray about what you are doing with your life. God can help you figure out your focus and priorities. Also, I want to recommend a fabulous book by Lysa TerKeurst called *The Best Yes: Making Wise Decisions in the Midst of Endless Demands.* This is a terrific, practical, best seller by one of my favorite women. Lysa dives deeply into this topic and gives you tons of practical strategies you can put in place to make sure you are living out The Best Yes!

Taking it Deeper:
How are you at saying no? Do you need to work on it? What is one thing you can say no to today? Let me gently encourage you to text that person and decline using one of your new tools. You'll be so glad you did!

Dealing With Difficult People

> *"Make sure that nobody pays back wrong for wrong, but always try to be kind to each other and to everyone else."* – 1 Thessalonians 5:15

I started at 9:00 am sharp, and the title of the seminar kind of said it all, "Dealing with Difficult People." This seminar usually drew people looking for creative ways to establish a more healthy work environment. I was looking forward to a fun, interesting and challenging day helping these people work out solutions and strategies.

In answer to my opening question, "Why are you here today?" an older man in the back row raised his hand. As I called on "Bud," I took a quick inventory. I noticed the deeply etched lines of discontent framing his down-turned mouth. His oversized hands were rough and callused and the wrinkles in his khaki work shirt mirrored those scored across his timeworn face. As he stood, he placed his hands on his hips, thrust out his chest and loudly proclaimed, "Well, I'm the difficult person, and I'm here today to find out what you're teaching, so when the people I work with try it on me, it won't work!" Hmmm... At least he was honest!

Does "Bud" sound familiar to you? Difficult People. Over the next few days we're going to consider some ideas for dealing effectively with them. I'm going to help you bring out the best in yourself first, then them, and even help you diffuse difficult interactions no matter who's at fault. Let's get started with a few questions.

When you encounter a difficult situation with a difficult person, ask:

1. Will this matter five years from now? How often have you reacted to something in the moment only to realize later that it really didn't matter in the big scheme of things? Yet your reaction left disrupted relationships and hurt feelings. Before you react, stop. Take a deep breath and ask yourself this perspective reminding question.

2. Who is getting the power here? Sometimes, believe it or not, these difficult people just want to throw the behavior, words, attitude out there to see how we react. (Interestingly, it's the same thing my 10 year old does when she wants to see me jump!) When we take the bait, we're giving them what they want. How about recognizing our reaction really gives them the power. Instead, let's stop, and ask...

3. How can I respond with the unexpected? When I was verbally accosted at the gas pump last week by the oversized 40-year-old-surfer-dude on his way to the lake, I just laughed. Based on his aggressive words, I'm sure he was looking for an argument. But the whole situation was so ridiculous, laughter was my only possible response. It stopped his aggression and I was left feeling slightly bemused rather than depleted by the incident.

Interestingly, these questions and behaviors are much easier to do with people you don't know. I think that's because we're so much more invested and connected with those in our close circle. It's that double whammy - we do what we don't want to with those closest to our hearts!

So try these ideas out on your family and co-workers and see what happens. Check back tomorrow for another set of strategies for dealing with difficult people.

Taking it Deeper:

How do you typically react to difficult people? What areas are you most sensitive to - and might react in the wrong way when squeezed? How can you implement any of these ideas described above?

More Strategies for Dealing with Difficult People

> *"Therefore each of you must put off falsehood and speak truthfully to his neighbor, for we are all members of one body."* – Ephesians 4:25

Previously, I gave you a few questions you could ask to get your mind into the right place when dealing with difficult people. They were:

1. Will this matter five years from now?
2. Who is getting the power here?
3. How can I respond with the unexpected?

By asking these questions, you will remind yourself to respond, not react when engaging with the difficult person. Now, let's take a look at our actual conversations.

Have you noticed that sometimes a person becomes difficult in reacting to something you innocently said to them? Well,

71

following are a few key ideas you can employ to make sure your communication is assertive without inducing defensiveness and anger.

1) **Focus on the problem, not the person.** For example, your co-worker Tara is consistently tardy to work three of five mornings a week. Her absence creates problems for you because when she's not there, you have to handle her workload as well as your own. Your tendency may be to focus on how irresponsible, lazy, and self-absorbed you think Tara is by her chronic tardiness. Instead, refocus and target the real problem here—don't make a judgement about her—just focus on her behavior and how it is affecting you. That way, when you talk with her about her behavior, you won't be accusatory; you'll just be able to focus on the facts of her behavior.

2) **Avoid absolutes and generalities.** Always, never, everyone, nobody, nothing, ever. Do those words sound familiar to you? Many of us are quick to assign an absolute and/or generality to a problem—like "Tara is always late." Or, how about, "Everyone knows you don't really care about your job." These statements are most likely incorrect, since few of us are always or never anything! They are also general—and will not help solve the situation. Stay specifically focused on the problem rather than create a defense response by throwing out glittering generalities and aggressive absolutes.

3) **Get specific.** Target the exact behavior that is bothering you. For example, instead of saying to Tara, "You're always late!" begin your discussion by saying "Yesterday, when you were 10 minutes late to work..." By getting specific about what you're talking

about, and letting them know precisely what you are having trouble with, you will keep the discussion on track and targeted. The more specific the better.

4) **Clearly state the specifics and tell them what you would like to see them change.** For example, your conversation with Tara might begin like this: "Tara, when you were 10 minutes late to work 3 times last week I felt really frustrated. I have had to cover my work as well as your own. It would really help me if you could be on time for work, or make arrangements for someone else to cover your duties until you arrive." Notice how specific that was? It had complete facts as well as what I wanted her to do differently.

There's so much we can talk about when it comes to clear, assertive communication to use especially when dealing with difficult people. I'm out of room for today, but tomorrow I'm going to give you a few more ideas. I'm so glad we're only 1/2 way through the month! There's so much more good stuff left to consider!

Taking it Deeper:
Do you have trouble speaking truthfully? What can you do to keep from using generalities and assumptions? What role does judgement have in your attitude towards others? How can you more clearly speak the truth in love?

Day 17

Difficult Conversations

"The wise in heart are called discerning, and pleasant words promote instruction." – Proverbs 16:21

We've been talking about ideas for dealing effectively with the difficult people in your life for the past few days. I hope you've gotten some useful ideas about how to get more positive outcomes. Today, I'm going to wrap up this section with a few extra suggestions.

I previously gave you an example of a dialogue with Tara. Today I'm going to give you a fresh dialogue along with some guidelines to follow when having that difficult conversation.

1) **Be honest with yourself.** When someone is difficult, check in and ask yourself, *what is the real issue here?* For example, if Mary made a sarcastic comment in front of your team about the way you're handling this month's project, your first reaction might be anger. But when you check in and are really honest, you'll

recognize that it was embarrassment and awkwardness you were experiencing in the moment. Additionally, when you were "put down" in front of your team, you might be worried it could potentially minimize your authority with them as well.

2) **Be willing to be authentically transparent.** Tell Mary the way her behavior affected you. You don't have to go into a huge long explanation here—and be careful NOT to insert judgements or generalities. Don't say, "Mary, you were a real jerk when you made that nasty comment about my work in front of my team this morning." That's NOT what we're looking for! Instead, say, "Mary, when you criticized my work in front of my team this morning I was really uncomfortable."

3) **Tell her what you want her to do.** Sometimes I'll hear people tell the difficult person they didn't appreciate the difficult behavior and then stop the conversation. Frankly, that does no good at all because most difficult people don't even get that their behavior is a problem! You must be specific and tell them what you want them to do. "Mary, in the future, when you have feedback on my work, I would appreciate it if you would tell me privately." Short, specific and without judgements should do the trick.

This conversation may seem hard to do. But rest assured, if you do not confront the difficult behavior it will continue. Remember, that which is rewarded is repeated. When you ignore their behavior it's a way of rewarding their behavior.

Be sure to draw your own firm assertive lines so you don't let the difficult people get the best of you.

Taking it Deeper:

Which of these suggestions have been most helpful to you? Which can you implement? What do you think about these straightforward conversations? Beneficial? Problematic? Why or Why not?

Gratitude

"And let the peace of Christ rule in your hearts, since as members of one body you were called to peace. And be thankful." – Colossians 3:15

For those of us in the United States, it's so easy to think and talk about gratitude during the month of November. Facebook posts are full of pithy sayings about being thankful, news coverage includes heartwarming stories of appreciation, and stereotypically heavy-laden church potlucks remind us of the sheer abundance of our lives.

Yet the challenge to be thankful is an ongoing one. In fact, the conflict of "not enough" comes screaming back full force just hours after the feast is over. For the past few years, the reminder of how we don't have enough is even creeping up on us earlier and earlier. (This year my newspaper and inbox were full of special sale ads starting about ten days before Thanksgiving.)

You know what I'm talking about don't you? "Black Friday" hits with the ferocity and intensity of Niagara Falls. Black Friday SHOUTS. I'm convinced its message is not really about the stuff though: I think it's deeper than that. It's the lie of the enemy that we not only don't have enough, indeed, we aren't enough.

And that's the tender spot isn't it? I believe the lie that if I just get that set of matching luggage, then I will be stylish enough. If I just load my kids down with that new doll/truck/game, then I will be a good enough mother. If I get my husband the latest tool, then I'll be a good enough wife. Oh, and if I will just be wise enough to take advantage of the incredible pricing on those things I really don't need, and don't have room for anyway, then I'll be a savvy enough homemaker. Oi vay! It's enough to make your head spin.

And that's what the father of lies wants, right? He wants me to spin my head from the truth, that none of that stuff matters because I am accepted and loved just as I am. The truth is that not one thing I do or say or buy will change my value. I already am enough.

Interestingly, it's the same lie I tell myself when my relationships start breaking down. The lie that my lack is why I can't fully connect. I imagine that if only I were more (fill in the blank) then we would become better leaders, managers, friends, co-workers, etc.

The truth is, it is when we are willing to recognize the lie for what it is (never fulfilling), and start being thankful for what we already have, that our relationships can start being repaired. In fact, it is only through gratitude that I am able to fully experience contentment and peace.

My prayer for you is peace through gratitude. When your sibling hurts your feelings, be thankful feelings will mend. When your parents give you unsolicited advice, be grateful you still have parents. When your kids misbehave, disobey and embarrass you, be thankful they are independent thinkers.

So today, in whatever season you find yourself, let's stop and take an inventory of all we already have. All we have in our relationships, our health, our work and indeed our lives. My hope is that our grateful hearts will realize just how full they already are.

Taking it Deeper:
Are you a grateful person? What are the things/people/events that pull you out of gratitude and into discontent? What steps can you take today to assure you stay in thankfulness? Write them down. Start.

Day 19

Words That Work

"A wise man's heart guides his mouth, and his lips promote instruction." – Proverbs 16:23

Words, words, magical words. It's amazing how the way we say things can impact our desired outcomes. As we have noticed over the past few days, what you say and the way you say it has a huge impact on your relationships.

Consider these two requests you might hear from a coworker: "Jennifer, I know you're really, really busy and have a lot on your plate, but if it's not too much trouble, and if you could maybe find the time, I could really use your help with this project if you think you might, maybe, be able to squeeze it into your crazy busy schedule."

Alternatively: "Jennifer, do you have five minutes? I would appreciate your input on this project." Which request would you be most inclined to answer in the affirmative? Obviously, the second. It's to the point, respectful and clear.

Many times, people think they are just being "nice" when they are actually unnecessarily using padded words and phrases that irritate, annoy and reduce the impact of their comment or request. Padded word and phrases have their appropriate uses— ask anyone married more than a year and they will agree to that—but in the workplace and as a communication rule, you will sabotage yourself if you routinely pad your words. You will be perceived as being insecure, indecisive and interestingly enough, even as a manipulator.

So, how do you stop padding? First, you want to edit your comments. If the word or phrase doesn't add value, omit it. Secondly, make sure you're choosing the most accurate words to convey your message. I suggest you even consider using power words and phrases. Consider the following lists of phrases and make note of those that seem familiar.

Words to Lose ~~ Padded Language
- "If it's not too much trouble..."
- "I know you're really busy, but... "
- "I really hate to bother you, but... "
- "You probably don't know the answer to this, but... "
- "I'm only the assistant, but I think... "
- "I know I'm the new person here, but... "
- "This is probably the wrong answer, but... "
- "It's only my opinion, but... "

Words to Use ~~ Power Phrases
- "I would like you to... "
- "Please finish this by... "
- "It would help me if you would... "
- "I suggest we... "

- "My experience has shown... "
- "Past practice indicates... "
- "The research points towards... "

And I'm sure you can add many more. Now that you're aware of the negative impact of padded words and phrases, I challenge you to be proactive in adding power phrases to your vocabulary. You'll be happy to watch your communication quotient soar.

> ### *Taking it Deeper:*
> Which padded words do you find yourself using? What words can you use that will be more effective? Which is more honest? Padding or Power Phrases?

Pass The Honey

"Gracious words are a honeycomb,
sweet to the soul and healing to the bones."
– Proverbs 16:24 (NIV)

Mama was right! She used to say, "You'll catch more flies with honey than vinegar." Manners are the honey that makes everything taste better. If you want to communicate more effectively and get what you want, need and expect, try a little honey. Here are some suggestions:

Remember the magic words:
"Please."
"Thank you."
"You're Welcome."

When someone sneezes, offer "Bless You," and then pass them a tissue.

When you pass someone in the hallway, say, "Excuse me."

In addition, the following list of simple kindnesses will sweeten things up in no time.

Respond to voice mails and emails in a timely manner. I was listening to old voicemails earlier in the week and almost had a heart attack when I heard a message left six weeks ago—to which I had failed to respond! Arghhhh!!! Have you noticed how easy it is to be rude in this technological world? Let's all be polite and respond promptly. If you have forgotten to respond, pick up the phone and call the person immediately to rectify as best you can. Using Facebook, Twitter, email, text messaging and cell phones properly can help you stay connected and communicating. Be sure to use them thoughtfully.

1) **Send notes in the mail.** Thank you notes. Congratulation notes. Thinking of You notes. These all work really well. My second job out of college (after leaving Capitol Hill) was as a Realtor. (Of course, one listing and one sale in one year does not a realtor make—I waited tables to pay my bills.) But one lasting lesson I learned during that time was from my real estate sales manager. He suggested I get in the habit of looking for articles of interest to my clients, then clip them and send them on with a little note. I did implement this idea, and I have continued it to this day.

   I do love it when I receive a little note, don't you? This week you can be the one to brighten someone's day with a well-written note.

2) **Lose the Profanity**. When I started doing Improv Comedy, I quickly learned that getting fast and easy laughs with off-color language and innuendo was never the better choice. It wasn't the potty humor that lasted; instead it was the richer, more difficult comedy

combinations that left the audience sated and replete from deep, tummy busting laughter.

Elevate your environment by eliminating the profanity and using better language.

So, put Mama's words into action. I'll look forward to hearing about your sweetened environments.

Taking it Deeper:

What's your favorite "honey" to use? When have you experienced the "honey" of others and how has it affected you? What can you do today to show a simple kindness?

Knowing Well

"So Joseph found favor in his sight and attended him, and he made him overseer of his house and put him in charge of all that he had." – Genesis 39:4 ESV

A common adage says, "People do business with those they know, like and trust." I'll re-vamp that to say people communicate best and most effectively with those they know, like and trust. So we're going to look at how you can grow in these three areas so you can have the positive communication with others you really want.

Know - How do you get to know others and get them to know you? The simplest answer is to be friendly. When you're in a new place, stick out your hand to someone you don't know, smile and say, "Hi, I'm (fill in your name)." This simple gesture opens the door to conversation, and soon you'll have a new connection. My college friend, George, reminds me that the very first time he ever met me was in our Speech 101 class when we were both 19. What he noticed was that I was "working the room," sticking out my hand, smiling and saying, "Hi, I'm Christy," as I met all my new "friends." Years later, he came to one of my daylong seminars and he just started laughing. "Christy," he chuckled, "You're still working the room." I smiled at him and said, "Yes, and still meeting lots of new friends!"

At work, everyone already knows you, but that doesn't mean you should stop being friendly. I've been in workplaces where the employees don't even acknowledge each other. There's no eye contact and rarely a smile. Needless to say, because they engage with each other solely when required, there's minimal relationship building and what's left is a building of strangers who work together only when absolutely required. I contend, if they were to take some time to get to know each other, their communication and their lives would be enriched in ways unimagined.

Oftentimes, people tell me they don't know what to talk about. So I'm going to recommend a favorite book that will help you with this challenge. It's a classic and was originally published in 1936! But like all classics, it's as fresh today as if it were written yesterday. It's called *How to Win Friends and Influence People* and I'm sure you know its author, Dale Carnegie. You may have heard that this book is full of tricky techniques to manipulate others into relationship with you. But I found just the opposite. Instead, it's all about how YOU can be a true friend to others. The magical outcome is that when you're a friend to others, others become your friend as well. I highly recommend this book!

Next, we'll talk about the other two parts of this discussion— how to build relationships so that people like and trust you. Until then, don't forget to be friendly!

Taking it Deeper:

Do you find it easy to be friendly, or do you have to work at this? What tips have you tried that makes it easier to stick out your hand and smile? What do you think Joseph did that allowed him to find favor?

Day 22

They Really Like Me

"So whatever you wish that others would do to you, do also to them, for this is the Law and the Prophets."
Matthew 7:12 ESV

Previously, we talked about how to become a person people want to communicate with because they know you. Building on the idea that people communicate most effectively with those they know, like and trust, let's dive a little deeper into the like and trust segments.

Like - Are you a likable person? What is that intangible that makes you like someone else? I think it's the magic of interest in others. When you are around someone who is genuinely interested in you, you can't help liking them. Their focus on you makes you feel good, and when you feel good, you're more likely to overlook minor irritants and like them back.

When I think of the people I really like, and want to know more, they are invariably people who are actually interested in me. And how do I know that? They ask questions. They listen when I answer them. They remember things about me and what is important to me. How are you doing? When was the last time you became more likable by asking thoughtful, interested questions? Why not start today?

Trust - Are you trustworthy? Do people know they can count on you no matter what? Trust is hard to build and very easy to lose. I know some people are slower to build trust than others, but the hard, cold fact is that nobody will take you seriously unless they can trust you. They need to know you will be ethical and do what you say you will do. Ouch.

My guess is most of us could improve in this area. Circumstances affect our behavior and sometimes we don't follow-through, or we allow ourselves to move in the shade of gray...hmmm. When others trust you, they have the gold standard to count on—and you have the privilege of being heard authentically when you communicate.

Know. Like. Trust. Three cornerstones for effective communication you can begin working on right now. If you are serious about building positive connections and living a purposeful life, you will want to think about and start putting into practice the skills of being known, likable and trustworthy.

Another excellent resource if you are struggling with this idea, is the book *Little Black Book of Connections: 6.5 Assets for Networking Your Way to Rich Relationships* by Jeffrey Gitomer. I love this book! It's fun and easy to read and most importantly, it's full of practical, actionable things you can do immediately to build connections. I think you'll like it too if you're looking for more help in this area.

Taking it Deeper:

What do the people you know, like and trust have in common? Can you name what element about them allows and encourages you to be in relationship with them?

Mama Knows Best

"The way of a fool is right in his own eyes, but a wise man listens to advice." – Proverbs 12:15 ESV

Famed football coach Vince Lombardi raised the football high enough so the whole team could see. Fearful yet hopeful eyes all stared up at him as he started their pre-season meeting with these words. "Gentlemen, this, is a football."

Sometimes you've just got to remember the basics. Today, let's take a peek at some basic and simple ideas for becoming a more positive communicator. In fact, these ideas are so basic and so simple, you may be able to say, as I do, "My mother really does know best!" See what you think...

1) **It's not what you say, it's how you say it.** Your tone, facial expressions, and body language all play a huge part in your communication (93% to be exact.) You may say, "Yes honey, I'd love to go to your office party with you." but your mate knows you're not telling the truth

because your rolling eyes, crossed arms and sarcastic tone all scream, "Of course I don't want to go be with your stupid co-workers for my one precious evening home this week!" Just be honest and match your non-verbal to your words for positive, effective communication.

2) **Actions speak louder than words.** If your manager asks you to do a project, and you say, "Sure, I'll do it," but somehow you never get around to actually doing it...be careful. Your actions (not doing the work) are speaking much louder than your words. You may think you're just keeping the peace and avoiding conflict, but be sure your actions will be the ultimate test in the end. Make sure your words and actions match.

3) **If you can't say something nice, don't say anything at all.** Saying ugly, negative things about people or situations does nobody any good; it just makes those around you uncomfortable. Make sure when you add a comment or idea that it is positive. A nice comment that benefits others. I loved being around my mother-in-law Shirley. She was consistently positive and in fact, at her memorial service, more than one person agreed with me, that we never heard her say a negative word about anybody. Now that's a testimony! I can only strive to be more like her.

4) **Only give advice when asked.** I've covered this extensively on Days 10 and 11, when I talked about giving unsolicited advice. If you need a refresher, be sure to take another look at those days. But I wanted to remind you in this list how important it is to keep your opinions to yourself if you want to build relationships and not walls. I know it's tempting to tell your 15-year-

old nephew that his permed, green, mop of hair is unattractive, but believe me, unless he asks for your input, he doesn't care what you think, and if you mention it, you will only succeed in building a barrier between the two of you. You never know when he will want someone to help him get it cut and re-dyed—a nice red or something—and if you have built a wall instead of a relationship, you'll miss out. No unsolicited advice!

Enjoy every moment as you build relationships remembering this handy list of ideas. And be sure to thank your Mother for her wisdom as well.

Taking it Deeper:

Which of these suggestions do you consistently follow? Which is the hardest for you to follow? Did you grow up hearing this advice or is it new to you? How can you pass this information along to the next generations?

Becoming a Master Communicator

> *"As iron sharpens iron, so one friend sharpens another."*
> – Proverbs 27:17

Tiger Woods, Michael Phelps, Ronald Reagan, Apolo Ohno, J.K. Rowling, Clive Cussler, Agatha Christie and Winston Churchill. What does this cast of characters have in common? The most obvious is that they all rose to the top of their profession and functioned at the top of their game under incredible pressure. Secondly, and most important to note, this august list of personalities practiced more than all the rest.

Tiger Woods was once asked by a fan to demonstrate how to hit the ball out of a sand trap. Tiger refused, saying he never practiced the wrong shot, only the right ones.

I am often asked how to get good at public speaking. My answer is always "Practice the right shot." And the right shot for speakers and communicators is Toastmasters.

Let me give you some background on this amazing organization and then share with you how to connect with a local club. Toastmasters began in California in 1924. Today it is an international non-profit organization boasting over 313,000 members in more than 14,650 clubs located in 126 countries. The one commonality of members is that each is committed to becoming a more effective communicator. The Toastmaster organization supports this common goal by providing a venue for members to hone their communication and leadership skills.

My own experience with Toastmasters was so positive I became a life-long advocate. Never have I been involved in a group as uplifting and positive towards each other. Good communication is not just about talking, it's about learning how to actively listen, respond and how to give good, productive feedback. By participating in the weekly meetings, you will learn how to do all of this and more.

My favorite story is about "Larry." My first visit to our local club was about week three for him. A part of each club meeting is a section called "Table Topics" when attendees are asked to stand up and speak impromptu on a given topic for 60 seconds. Poor Larry was so scared and nervous and freaked out when it was his turn, he stood, hands glued tightly to the back of the chair, chin tucked firmly upon his chest and whispered, stumbling and stuttering through his speech topping out at about 45 seconds of torture. I hurt for him!

Fast forward 12 months. This time when Table Topics was called, Larry stood confidently. He looked around the room as he spoke. He used humor. He used voice inflection. His impromptu speech sounded like it had been planned and fine-tuned for weeks. He not only nailed that activity, but he won the weekly award for best Table Topic! Talk about a turnaround! That's what Toastmasters does for you.

That's why, if you are serious about becoming a Master Communicator you need to get yourself to a local Toastmasters club, join, and start reaping the benefits of this connection. On a side note...each club has its own "flavor." So if you don't feel comfortable at the first club you visit, find another to try out. Even the smallest of communities usually have several clubs to choose from, so you're sure to find one that's a fit for you.

Taking it Deeper:
Have you ever visited a Toastmasters club?
What was your experience? What are some
other ways to find opportunity to practice your
communication skills?

Day 25

Communicating L.O.V.E

"Do not judge, or you too will be judged. For in the same way you judge others, you will be judged, and with the measure you use, it will be measured to you. Why do you look at the speck of sawdust in your brother's eye and pay no attention to the plank in your own eye? How can you say to your brother, 'Let me take the speck out of your eye,' when all the time there is a plank in your own eye? You hypocrite, first take the plank out of your own eye, and then you will see clearly to remove the speck from your brother's eye." – Matthew 7:1-5

Why is is that we often treat the people we love the most in the very worst way? Or am I the only one? I'm betting I'm not. Yet when I think over what makes a life truly well lived, I realize it all boils down to how well we get along, engage with and yes, even love our family and friends. Therefore, following is an acrostic with my suggestions for how to really communicate L.O.V.E.

Laughter: Giggle, chuckle, guffaw...laugh until you cry! Tell funny stories from your past; remembering that Christmas when you were six years old and Great Aunt Georgina "fell asleep" in the mashed potatoes, is fun for everyone (except Great Aunt Georgina of course!). Pull out old photo albums and laugh at how dorky you looked in 7th grade. Watch *Planes, Trains and Automobiles;* that's a movie guaranteed to tickle your funny bone. Families and friends who laugh together...have fun! Laughter is the best medicine and does your heart good. (Trite but true.) And of course, remember that when the dog rolls in the newly planted flower bed, your daughter spills honey all over your freshly cleaned floors and you sew the costume inside out and backwards 1 hour before the party starts, these incidents will be fodder for family laughs for years to come. Laughing together communicates love.

Other Focus: A wise teacher told me long ago that true Joy comes when you put others before yourself. I would encourage you to try this. Let go of focusing on what you want and re-focus on what others need. When I focus on me, me, me, I become discontent, disappointed and depressed. Comparing my insides to some else's outsides just makes it worse. But when I let go of myself, focus on others and how I can impact them in a positive way, my whole paradigm shifts! Focusing on others communicates love.

(I must include a whole paragraph of warning to the "O" suggestion. Oftentimes I see mothers get so wrapped up in their kid's and husband's needs they ignore their own. Please don't do this! What I'm suggesting is a healthy balance. Focus not only on your family and not only on yourself...but a balance. Make sure each day has a little of both. In the mother's life, it's a tricky balance of both isn't it? Please remember that sometimes serving yourself is the best way to serve others.)

Vorgiveness...err...Forgiveness: Please let go of that baggage that's holding you back. Your anger and resentment are only hurting you. In the words Frozen made famous...Let it Go! There is a scene in the movie, *The Piano* where Holly Hunter is being pulled to a watery grave by tangled ties holding her to a piano plummeting to the bottom of the ocean. It isn't until she decides to break free (let go) of the heavy ropes and unburden herself from the weight of the piano that she is able to kick her way up through the water to the life-giving air at the surface. The next time you are tempted to hold on to that resentment, I urge you to let go instead and communicate love.

Expect the Best: What you are looking for is looking for you. We have a joke in my family that I get all the green lights and my husband gets all the red lights. I'm sure, we have statistically the same experience, but our perception of who gets what is definitely affected by our outlook. I celebrate my (expected) greens while my husband suffers through his (expected) reds. I wonder which you would rather experience? When you expect fighting, animosity and negativity, that's exactly what you will find. Expect the best and you will communicate love.

Taking it Deeper:
So how about it? Today can you communicate L.O.V.E. by implementing some of these ideas? What do you think keeps you from implementing these suggestions? What are some things you can do right now?

How to Give It—Giving Feedback

> *"Each of you should look not only to your own interests, but also to the interests of others."*
> – Philippians 2:4

Communicating what you really think or feel is part of everyday life. Doing it with finesse and tact is a skill you can learn to master. Giving and receiving feedback is an especially important part of communication. Today we will talk about giving feedback and tomorrow about receiving feedback.

When you are Giving Feedback:

1) **Be Specific.** When someone is having difficulty with getting their work turned in on time, say, "I've noticed that in February, March and April your reports were turned in two days late each month." Not, "So, looks like you're really busy these days." The first was specific about the real issue, while the second left the listener wondering what you're really saying.

2) **Avoid Assumptions.** When you make an assumption like, "I know you probably don't like discussing this issue, but..." it puts people on the defensive. When we assume, we're taking upon ourselves the projected thoughts of another. Many times we're way off base! Who really knows the mind of another? Instead, say, "I would like to discuss our report schedule. Do you have time now or later in the afternoon?" This gets the conversation going on an even, unbiased note.

3) **Avoid Generalities.** The minute you say, "Everyone knows you're always late with your reports," not only does the person become defensive, but you've set yourself up to be disagreed with from the beginning of the conversation. After all, who among us is "always" or "never" anything? Keep yourself focused on solutions by being specific and targeted in your discussion.

4) **Focus on the Problem, not the Person.** Our tendency is to personalize issues. When I complain about Ariel being selfish and uncommitted to the team because she's always late coming back from her breaks, I'm not only making an assumption and generalization, I'm also targeting Ariel, personally with my words, not focusing on her behavior. When I focus on the problem—that is that other team members can't take their breaks when Ariel is late returning from her break—the focus keeps me from getting personal and/or attacking her. This helps the conversation stay in productive territory. Remember, when I target the behavior, then I can ask for that behavior to change for the better.

So, the next time you have to give feedback, I hope you remember these suggestions so that your conversation is productive, encouraging and keeping you on the path of creating positive connections and helping you developing deeper relationships.

> ### *Taking it Deeper:*
> Do you ever have trouble staying specific and focusing on the problem, not the person? Do you find it easy to get personal? What can you do to keep from making personal attacks?

Day 27

How to Take It—Receiving Feedback

"Listen to advice and accept instruction, that you may gain wisdom in the future." – Proverbs 19:20 ESV

I previously discussed giving feedback with tact and professionalism. Now, I want to give you some suggestions for receiving feedback in the most productive way.

When Receiving Feedback:

1) **Ask for clarification.** What's your response when your boss says, "You don't seem to care much about your job these days." Do you get defensive and react or do you take a deep breath and ask for clarification like this... "What am I doing that gives you that impression?" Asking for clarification is a good way to slow down the conversation and get it headed in a more productive direction.

2) **Ask for specifics.** When your coworkers says, "You're really trying to get on the boss's good side," rather than

reacting with a sarcastic or cutting response, just turn it around and ask, "Oh, what makes you say that?" You'll shut her negativity down without engaging in any of your own.

3) **Respond, don't react.** Sometimes people give us feedback that we weren't expecting. When you give yourself space to respond, you're setting yourself up for success. A sentence like "I'd like to think about what you just said and get back with you about it later this afternoon," is perfectly acceptable and preferable to an angry reaction. You dictate how you will engage with someone. Don't give your power away to them.

4) **Expect the positive.** One time I was speaking to a group of trucking executives in Montana. Throughout the day I noticed one man in the front row who seemed to visibly disagree with everything I said. During one interactive time, I asked, "What is it? You obviously don't agree with me." "Oh, no!" he exclaimed, "I was just thinking how much I agree with you and that you were hitting on everything that was going wrong with my company. I've been thinking of all the ways I could fix the problems." Oh my. I had completely misread his body language and because I had been expecting the worst (based on what I saw) I was expecting a negative response. What a great lesson. Look for, and expect, the best. Most of the time, it's out there, just waiting for you to discover it.

5) **Give grace.** Sometimes people spout off without thinking, giving you feedback that should have much more prudently gone unspoken. If that happens to you, I'd encourage you to just skip it and forget it. Life is too short to nurse grudges against people who have said ugly

things to you. Just this morning I had to give myself this very advice as one of my clients spoke extremely rudely and aggressively to me. My feelings were hurt. And then I remembered that I would be better off to give him grace and just let it go. All of us have some days that are better than others. By giving grace you allow others the freedom for a not-so-perfect day...and who knows, maybe next time you'll be the one on the receiving end of the grace-giving.

Taking it Deeper:

How good are you at accepting feedback? Is it easy for you or do you, (like I), get defensive? Write down a story of when you received grace from someone. How does that make you feel? What's the real benefit to you of really hearing and absorbing when someone gives you feedback?

Day 28

Live Generously

"They are to do good, and to be rich in good works, to be generous and ready to share, thus storing up treasure for themselves as a good foundation for the future, so that they may take hold of that which is truly life."
– 1 Timothy 6:18-19

"Greatness is not defined by what a person receives, but by what a person gives." John Maxwell. Have you noticed that the people you most like to communicate with, (be around) are generous of words, actions and spirit? I have written often of "Giving Grace" to other, of thinking well of others and of speaking words that benefit. I want to share with you some ideas I got from John Maxwell's book, *Today Matters: 12 Daily Practices to Guarantee Tomorrow's Success* (Maxwell, John C.). His chapter on Generosity really hit me on the head, and I think you will like his ideas too.

1) **Choose Generosity.** J. Paul Getty was known for being the richest man in the world. He was also known as one of the most stingy…even refusing to pay ransom when a grandson got kidnapped! By the time he died in 1976 he had alienated all his children as well as his five former wives. Contrast that with Dave Thomas of Wendy's fame. He was known for being generous of spirit with himself as well as his money. Over his lifetime he gave away millions of dollars, as well as hours and hours of his time and passion in his interest of helping others. He said, "Share your success and help others succeed. Give everyone a piece of the pie. If the pie's not big enough, make a bigger pie." Which person would you like to model yourself after? You get to choose. Choose generosity.

2) **Value People.** Think of what you love. Your home, your car, your toys. I'll bet you spend time and money maintaining these items. What about the people you value? Why is it so easy to pursue the things we love instead of the people we love? (I actually think the answer to that is a whole different book!) Find ways to value people. The best and simplest is to listen to them. Spend time with them. Help them feel heard. I was listening to a podcast recently and the speaker challenged us to "add energy" in our every encounter. When you leave someone, is their energy higher or lower? You can be an energy giver or and energy taker. You get to choose. Choose—every day in every way I will add value to others.

3) **Do It Every Day.** "Do all the good you can, to all the people you can, in all the ways you can as long as you can," D. L. Moody. Don't wait for your income or

circumstances to change—just begin! Science is now showing how our behavior impacts our mind. Living generously will make us generous people. Dr. Martin Luther King Jr. said, "Life's most persistent and urgent question is, 'what are we doing for others?'" Choose to act generously every day.

My friend, Amy Sullivan, has written a wonderful book to help you teach generosity to yourself and your kids. The title, *When More is Not Enough - How to Stop Giving Your Kids What They Want and Give Them What They Need* really says it all. Tons of creative ideas are found here. Additionally, my friend, Courtney DeFeo has a terrific program she created called "Light 'Em Up". Check it out on her website:

www.courtneydefeo.com.

Designed to be done with your kids, it's a great way to teach by doing. Oh, and it's fun!

Let me leave you today with a thought from Ann Voskamp, "When someone stops doing nothing, and just starts doing something, this is what starts to change everything." Today is your day. Start.

Taking it Deeper:
Is it difficult for you to be generous? How do you motivate yourself to choose generosity? What are a few ways you can show generosity this month?

Day 29

Your Communication Style

"Though I am free and belong to no man, I make myself a slave to everyone, to win as many as possible...To the weak I became weak, to win the weak. I have become all things to all men so that by all possible means I might save some."
– 1 Corinthians 9:19 and 22

What kind of communicator are you? Passive? Aggressive? Or the gold standard, Assertive?

I'm going to give you a quick overview so you can evaluate if you are where you want to be and/or if maybe your style is getting in the way of your effectiveness in building positive connections and creating a life of purposeful living.

Passive Communicator: Someone who has a reluctance and/ or inability to confidently express what they think and feel.

This person is quiet, shy and rarely says what they really think or feel. They will keep their thoughts to themselves, often taken extreme amounts of time to think about what they will say before they say it. They expect you to read their mind since they have limited body language and minimal facial expressions.

My favorite story about passive communicators happened when I was speaking in Minot, North Dakota. I had a group of 40 women in my "Powerful Communication Skills for Women" class. The majority of them were of Scandinavian descent— internal processors and typically passive communicators.

Throughout the day, I was getting basically no visible response from them. I would say something funny and they would crack a slight smile or barely nod their heads. As someone who gets their energy from other people, all day long I was giving myself pep talks, reminding myself that they were engaging on the inside, even if I couldn't see much evidence on the outside. At the end of the day I was shaking hands at the door saying goodbye. One after another of the women told me how much they loved the class. One woman generously proclaimed, "This was the best class I've ever attended." "Oh, thank you," I replied. "Yes," she continued. "My favorite part was how you got us all so involved!" Inside my head, I was screaming, "When? I missed it!"

That's a funny story, but it illustrates the difficulty others can have with passive communicators. Because passive communicators tend to keep everything inside, others can be at a loss to know their real feelings. They are also very good at using passive aggressive manipulation to get what they want. (I think passive-aggressive behavior is a thought for another day.)

Aggressive Communicator: A person who intimidates, demeans and degrades another person—they exhibit behavior that results in a put-down, causing defensiveness and hurt.

You've meet these aggressive communicators. They are intent on getting their way and letting you know it. The classic aggressive communicator can be found on the schoolyard—we call him a bully. Or maybe she's the one in your daughter's peer group who is the dominate force. She tells all the other girls what they should do and how they should do it. An out of control aggressor uses their threat of anger to manipulate those around her.

The Aggressive Communicator uses their body language with their hands on their hips, their finger pointing at you (while they shake their hand) and the scowl on their face to get their messages across.

Assertive Communicator: This person confidently expresses what they think, feel and believe. They stand up for their rights while respecting the rights of others.

You love these people. They know what they want and they share it assertively. When you finish a conversation with this assertive person, you feel great! Encouraged and energized because you have been on the receiving end of healthy, life-affirming communication.

So, which kind of communicator are you? By nature, most of us fall into either passive or aggressive. Most of us have to *learn* how to be an assertive communicator. It helps if your family of origin used good, healthy communication. But even if they were too far on either end, you can learn to communicate assertively with practice and diligent effort.

Taking it Deeper:
Which category do you fall into? What challenges have you experienced with your own natural style? How have you worked around your style to get better results?

Strategies To Say It Right The First Time

"Do not let any unwholesome talk come out of your mouths, but only what is helpful for building others up according to their needs, that it may benefit those who listen." – Ephesians 4:29

The information age has inundated us with...you've got it. Information. Some is awesome. Some is irritating. Some is just plain stupid. And sometimes that's how it us with us. We talk. And talk. And some of what we say is awesome, some irritating and some downright stupid.

In light of the overload most of us constantly feel, I thought it would be helpful and refreshing for us to consider how we can be effective in telling people our thoughts and ideas in a way that's "right the first time." So here for your consideration are three suggestions to help you do just that.

1) **Be respectful of the person.** The next time your employee suggests an idea you think is ridiculous—remember to focus your response on the idea, not the person. As you are respectful of the person, get specific with your responses to the idea, so they know you are skeptical of the idea, not them as an employee.

2) **Get to the point.** Head right to the comment without padding it with extra words or fillers like um, and, ahh, so, like, etc. The more you add needless words to what you are saying, the more likely you are to lose your listener and undermine your credibility.

3) **Make suggestions for improvement instead of criticizing.** Many years ago I had a speaking coach who would intentionally sit in on my program and then make suggestions on how I could improve. Her way of suggesting improvements was fabulous. She used the "Like best" and "Next time" technique. First, she would tell me what she liked best about the program. Then she would say, "Christy, next time, instead of telling that joke at the beginning of the program, tell it at the end." By using the like best and next time method, I could hear what was working and what wasn't working. The bonus was that I did not get defensive at the criticism, because I heard ways to improve…and that is what I really wanted all along anyway.

All through the year, I know we have lots of opportunities to practice communicating with people who are really important to us. I hope you can stick these three additional ideas into your communication toolbox and whip them out the next time you need to say it right the first time.

Taking it Deeper:

Which of these are most difficult for you to do? Do you ever gotten stuck when you didn't know what to say, so you said nothing? Have you experienced someone else doing these things for you? How did it feel?

Day 31

Why Are We Working On This Stuff Anyway?

"Instead, speaking the truth in love, we will in all things grow up into him who is the Head, that is, Christ. From him the whole body, joined and held together by every supporting ligament, grows and builds itself up in love, as each part does its work." – Ephesians 4:15-16

I'm writing this last devotional while sitting in the Emergency Room. I'm here because my 89-year-old father-in-law was unresponsive, then confused this morning when they got him up at the Veteran's Home where he lives. I'm waiting while they draw his blood, look inside of him with CT scans, X-rays and then analyze the results to figure out what's going on.

And I guess there's really nothing like a drama with a loved one to remind you why we're doing all this communication stuff in the first place.

I can give you all kinds of tips and techniques on how to be a more effective communicator. But the bottom line reason we learn and do all this is so we can love each other better. Right? We want to learn how to act and speak and express ourselves in the best way possible so that the people in our lives feel loved.

Does that make sense to you? Who in your life do you wish knew how much you loved them? Do you communicate that love? What's getting in the way of your truth? This morning I'm drawn to think of this…and here are the two main questions I'm asking myself.

1) **Is my style getting in the way of my message?** Earlier I wrote about being a passive, aggressive or assertive communicator. That message was straight from my heart. You see, I am really strong. I come across as strong. I have to work hard to dial down from aggressive to assertive, and sometimes even assertive is too much. And sometimes that 'natural style' is getting in the way of my message.

When I'm trying to talk with my daughter Amelia or husband Tom about something I'm passionate about (almost everything), I think I get too wound up and my words, tone, body all end up sending messages that actually shut them down. Do you have that challenge? Or do you go the other way, and you shut down when you get passionate? I think both of these can be a challenge. I have to remember, it's not all about me…it's about communicating well. Because, I LOVE THEM.

2) **Do I find ways to communicate love even when I'm stressed and busy and overwhelmed?** When I think of all the times I've thought of my telling my mother something and not texted her, or bragged about my sister

and not called her, or even been angry with my dad and talked about him instead of talking with him, it makes my heart sad. I'm supposed to be teaching this stuff! Instead, I so often fail in the execution of the communication.

How about you? Would it help your relationships if you were more intentional communicating your love to those in your life? I want to take each opportunity to communicate love and not put it off until later. Because, as I'm being so forcibly reminded today, there's no guarantee of tomorrow, and I want to rest assured I'm communicating my love the best possible way every day.

> **Taking it Deeper:**
> Does today's discussion ring true with you? Are you doing things that grow your relationships with clear, loving communication? How can you do that more?

I've given you 31 specific ideas on how to be more effective with positive communication. I hope you will take these ideas and move yourself into the assertive category. Your friends, family and co-workers will thank you, and you'll be empowered knowing you can use these tools to create a life of strong, active and relationship building communication. Here's our take-away: Let's commit together to using positive communication to create positive relationships so that we can live purposeful lives. I think we'll all be glad we did.

Afterword

You did it! You've taken the time to work through 31 specific ideas on how to be more effective as a positive communicator. I hope you will take these ideas put them into practice. Together, let's commit to using positive communication to create positive relationships so that we can live purposeful lives.

What was your favorite skill? I'd suggest you write the basic concept on a 3x5 card and tape it to your bathroom mirror, or stick it inside your wallet or on the console of your car. Think about it and work on it daily until it becomes more natural to you. Then pick another and start on that!

It's never ending isn't it? But as our kindergarten teachers told us, "practice makes perfect" and to become a better communicator, you must practice, practice, practice. If you would like to continue this journey together, be sure to check out all the resources I have available at my website, **www.christylargent.com**.

Thank you, thank you, thank you for reading through this far! As my way of saying double-thanks, I have a gift for you. If you go to my website, **www.christylargent.com/31resources**, you will find a resource guide I've put together just for you. It's a compilation of the 31 best communication resources to be found today. Using this tool, you can take what we've started with here and go even deeper.

I'd love to get your feedback, so be sure to leave me a comment on my website or shoot me an email at **christylargentspeaker@gmail.com**.

Visit me on Facebook: **Facebook.com/ ChristyLargentSpeaker**

Visit me on Twitter: **twitter.com/ChristyLargent**

Visit me on Instagram: **instagram.com/christylargent**

Visit me on Pinterest: **pinterest.com/christylargent**

Can You Help?

Review
Thanks so much for reading my book! I really appreciate it and I love hearing what you have to say.

So, with that in mind, I need your input to make the next version of this book even better.

Please leave a helpful REVIEW on Amazon.
Thanks so much!

Christy

List of Biblical Verses Used

Day 1	1 Corinthians 10:31-33
Day 2	Philippians 2:3
Day 3	1 Corinthians 4:19
Day 4	Proverbs 31:26
Day 5	Proverbs 15:1
Day 6	Colossians 4:6
Day 7	Philippians 4:8
Day 8	James 1:19
Day 9	Proverbs 1:5
Day 10	Proverbs 23:9
Day 11	Proverbs 18:2
Day 12	1 Thessalonians 5:16-18
Day 13	James 1:5
Day 14	Philippians 4:6-7
Day 15	1 Thessalonians 5:15
Day 16	Ephesians 4:25
Day 17	Proverbs 16:21
Day 18	Colossians 3:15
Day 19	Proverbs 16:23
Day 20	Proverbs 16:24
Day 21	Genesis 39:4
Day 22	Matthew 7:12
Day 23	Proverbs 12:15
Day 24	Proverbs 27:17
Day 25	Matthew 7:1-5
Day 26	Philippians 2:4
Day 27	Proverbs 19:20
Day 28	1 Timothy 6:18-19
Day 29	1 Corinthians 9:19 and 22
Day 30	Ephesians 4:29
Day 31	Ephesians 4:15-16

About the Author

Christy Largent is a humorist, professional speaker, podcaster, blogger, TV host, and most importantly, wife and mother of two children adopted from China. She is passionate about helping people realize their potential by showing them how to live purposeful, positive lives of meaningful connection.

For almost 20 years, her message has enabled people to:

- Communicate competently and confidently in every situation.
- Replace negative self-talk and destructive self-sabotage with self-confidence and a path for positive promotion
- Discover how to embrace their innate strengths and maximize with joy the unique aspects of their personality.
- Develop a focused and grateful purpose so that they can live the lives they were born to live.

Christy lives in small town northern California with her husband Tom and 2 young children. Please join Christy and discover how fun and rewarding positive communication can really be! Visit **www.christylargent.com** or check out her weekly podcast, **Encouraging Words for Working Moms**.

Made in the USA
San Bernardino, CA
19 August 2015